LETTS POCKET GUIDE TO

DOGS

Choosing and caring for
your pet. Over 100 breeds
described and illustrated in colour

Beverley Cuddy and Chris Bell

Front cover illustration: Airedale Terrier

This edition first published in 1994
by Charles Letts & Co Ltd
Letts of London House,
Parkgate Road
London SW11 4NQ

'Letts' is a registered trademark of
Charles Letts & Co Limited

This edition produced by
Malcolm Saunders Publishing Ltd, London

© 1994 Malcolm Saunders Publishing Ltd

A CIP Catalogue record for this book is available
from the British Library

ISBN 1 85238 438 7

Printed in Spain

Contents

Introduction

This is a book for people who want to know more about dogs. It is a stepping stone to more detailed breed-specific works or to experts on particular breeds.

The dog has been man's best friend for 10,000 years, but the cult of the pedigree dog in the last few centuries has made the decision about which one to own quite baffling, as the selection is so enormous.

You can predict the ultimate size, shape, coat and temperament tendencies of a pedigree pup and there is a dog to suit nearly every person's requirements. However, some people's lives are much too busy or complicated to include a dog. Often, a cat will prove the perfect solution for them. This book provides you with the information to help you reach that decision.

How to use this book

The book starts with the smallest breeds and ends with the giants. The order is determined by height at the shoulder. In nearly every breed, the female is smaller than the male, sometimes by a very large margin. The height referred to should be taken as a rough guide as it is the tallest figure quoted in the breed standard (the Kennel Club's blueprint for breed perfection). Some breed standards do not give an ideal height, in those cases we quote a weight, if known. The height or weight reference is given in the coloured band at the top of each page.

Each breed recognized by the British Kennel Club is allocated to one of six groups, which are given below. These classifications are meant to link breeds of similar purpose, but there are lots of ambiguities so the group label should not be given too great a significance. In other countries, some breeds are classified into different groups.

TOY

Small companion dogs. Some members of the group, for example the Yorkshire Terrier, have done a job in the not too distant past. Generally very easy to live with as they have been bred for centuries as pets.

HOUND

Breeds which helped man to hunt either by sight or scent. The sight hounds (for example the Greyhound) usually still have a tendency to chase, so can be difficult with cats. The scent hounds (for example the Basset Hound) will often have a lot of their brains in their nose.

TERRIER

Most terrier breeds go to ground after prey. Man further refined some breeds to bait large animals or fight other dogs. The terrier spirit is brave, tenacious and independent. Most will like digging, games of tug-of-war and toys that squeak.

UTILITY

This is the group into which the Kennel Club puts breeds that don't fit elsewhere. The Poodle, for example, was originally a gundog but ended up here. The Standard Schnauzer is in the Working group but his two smaller cousins joined the misfits department, which includes in its range the Bulldog, Akita and Dalmatian.

WORKING

The largest group. Herding dogs, guards, rescue dogs and any breed that helps man to work. The working dogs tend to be intelligent, quick to learn and very biddable. However, working instincts can be very strong and sometimes this makes them unsuitable as pets. For example, a Border Collie is perfectly happy working all day. Deny that brain something to work on and he will round up your children — or even your furniture!

GUNDOG

Close behind the invention of the firearm came the creation of the gundog. Hunting, pointing, springing and retrieving game are the main functions. Some breeds are good all-rounders, others expert at one skill. Gundogs are usually intelligent dogs needing lots of stimulation. Some do not fit many domestic circumstances.

Specimen page

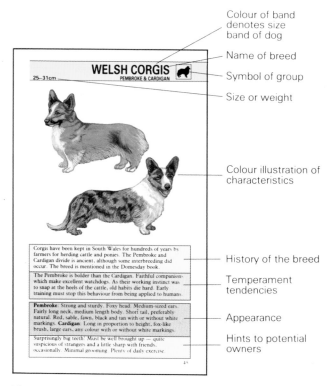

Colour of band denotes size band of dog

Name of breed

Symbol of group

Size or weight

Colour illustration of characteristics

History of the breed

Temperament tendencies

Appearance

Hints to potential owners

WELSH CORGIS
PEMBROKE & CARDIGAN

25–31cm

Corgis have been kept in South Wales for hundreds of years by farmers for herding cattle and ponies. The Pembroke and Cardigan divide is ancient, although some interbreeding did occur. The breed is mentioned in the Domesday book.

The Pembroke is bolder than the Cardigan. Faithful companions which make excellent watchdogs. As their working instinct was to snap at the heels of the cattle, old habits die hard. Early training must stop this behaviour from being applied to humans.

Pembroke: Strong and sturdy. Foxy head. Medium-sized ears. Fairly long neck, medium length body. Short tail, preferably natural. Red, sable, fawn, black and tan with or without white markings. **Cardigan**: Long in proportion to height, fox-like brush, large ears, any colour with or without white markings.

Surprisingly big teeth. Must be well brought up — quite suspicious of strangers and a little sharp with friends, occasionally. Minimal grooming. Plenty of daily exercise.

Knowing your dog

Once you have located your dog you will find its size given in the coloured band at the top of the page. This is expressed in height or weight (see above). Then four boxes provide information about your dog as follows:

History of the breed

Most breeds of dog were bred for a purpose and the short history section given on each page will give an insight into this. For example, if you can't choose between a Cavalier King Charles Spaniel and Border Terrier, a look at their origins would tell you which one is the purpose-built lap dog. Unfortunately dog history is quite patchy, and much of it relies on word-of-mouth. Experts within a breed will disagree and this book attempts to give only basic historical information. Some early visual breed history does exist. The rich were likely to have portraits painted with their pets, but little remains of the working man and his devoted companion. Should the short passage give you a taste for more, most breeds have several in-depth books written about them.

Temperament tendencies

We all know that temperament is not just inherited, it is shaped by upbringing and early environment. However, it is possible to paint a broad picture of any temperament tendencies a breed may have. Some dogs are more biddable than others, some independent and aloof. For example a Chow Chow loves to bond with one person yet a Golden Retriever will be a friend to the whole family. Temperament traits often relate to the original function that the dog was bred for. If you are a first-time owner, a dog which has been bred as a pet for generations will provide much less of a challenge than one which prefers to work all day.

Appearance

For every breed of dog there is a very wordy breed standard — a canine blueprint. It details every aspect of the way a dog should look from nose to tail. Our section attempts to comment on the most important points that give the dog its individual look. If a breed has previously been customarily docked we note it in this section.

Hints to potential owners

This is the most important part of the book. It tells you things you should know before you buy. For example, it gives you an idea of potential problems with grooming, training, exercise and health. We'd much rather you knew about potential hereditary problems so you can find a responsible breeder who is doing all he can to eradicate them.

Selecting a dog

There are hundreds of different pedigree breeds of dog and an infinite variety of mongrels and crossbreeds to choose from. Selecting the perfect pet can be bewildering and it's easy to make the wrong choice. This book is designed to be your guide, helping you draw up your shortlist and pointing you in the right direction for more information. Not every breed has been covered in this guide, but all the most popular varieties are included, together with some of the more exotic.

Before you get anywhere near a cute, fluffy puppy, take a very close look at your lifestyle. There is a type of dog to suit most people, but sometimes a cat or a goldfish is the only animal which will fit your routine. You should pick a breed which suits your life and not fool yourself into believing you can change to suit the dog.

Try not to select a dog on appearance alone, the novelty of a long coat or a wrinkly face will soon wear off. Let the personality, exercise requirement and original purpose the dog was bred for influence your decision.

Mongrels and crossbreeds

While this book concentrates on pedigree dogs, mongrels and crossbreeds can make wonderful pets. Some people say mongrels are healthier and more intelligent than their blue-blooded brothers as there is less chance of hereditary disease. The genes that cause many of these problems are recessive and will usually not be shared by parents of mixed breeds.

However, there are some drawbacks with opting for a non-pedigree dog. It is much more difficult to predict the ultimate size, coat-type and temperament of a dog from mixed parentage. But, if the mother can be seen, at least half the information is known. It can be quite difficult to find well-reared non-pedigree pups. You should avoid pet shops and either go to your local rescue sanctuary or find a local litter brought up in a busy, household environment by people you trust.

Where to buy a pedigree puppy

The ideal person to buy a dog from is someone who is going to ask you lots of awkward questions. If a breeder will only sell their puppy to the best possible home, you can usually assume they will have had the pup's welfare at heart all through the rearing of the litter.

Avoid people who breed for profit alone. Symptoms of a 'puppy farmer' or 'puppy dealer' are many different breeds for sale, or lots of litters. If the mother of the litter is not available for you to meet, go elsewhere. Many litters are farmed in rural areas and transported into more densely populated areas for re-sale. Dogs from puppy farms can be more prone to disease and are often very traumatized by their long journey. Even though you may feel sorry for one of these pups, to buy one just encourages the trade to continue. A good breeder will be a source of help and advice throughout your dog's lifetime.

Every breed has an association formed by enthusiasts who really care about the health and well-being of their favourite type of dog. The Kennel Club should be able to give you their address and phone number. The breed club secretary should put you in contact with breeders in your area.

Kennel Club registration
Some people believe Kennel Club registration is a mark of quality. This is not correct — Kennel Club registration is the equivalent of a human birth certificate. If you want to show your dog or breed from it, you must make sure the breeder has registered the puppy you buy and either passes the registration to you with the puppy or gives you a written assurance that it will be forwarded to you.

Taking on a rescued dog
If you might consider an older dog needing a new home, the Kennel Club produces a rescue directory, listing who to contact for nearly every breed of dog. More and more people are choosing to take on a rescued dog. There are thousands of unwanted pets sitting in kennels waiting for a new owner to come and take them home.

When visiting a rescue centre, give a thought to the dogs that are usually last to be chosen. Small white dogs are always popular, but brown or black dogs are seldom selected. You need to ask to see the Lurchers and Greyhounds. They don't like the cold so will usually cuddle up in their beds while prospective owners walk past oblivious.

They can make excellent pets for all sorts of people, and they need much less exercise and space than people imagine.

Older dogs are also slow to be 're-homed', which is a great pity as they are usually perfectly trained and unused to kennel life.

Choose a dog that fits your needs. If you have children, pick the dog that comes forward wagging its tail. If you have a quiet lifestyle, the one at the back looking shy may grow into the perfect companion with one-to-one care and lots of love.

Dog or bitch?

Whether to have a male or female dog will normally come down to personal choice. In some breeds the male may be very macho, but in others the biggest problem is that the stud dogs are so lacking in libido that the breed's future is threatened! If you choose to have your pet neutered, both dog and bitch will be equally easy to live with. There are now injections which can control a bitch's seasons or suppress the male's urges to wander after bitches in season. Many dogs and bitches from rescue sanctuaries will already be neutered.

Early training

The importance of socialization

The early weeks of a puppy's life are very important. The trainers at the Guide Dogs for the Blind Association were the first to realize that if a puppy doesn't learn about the world before it is 14 weeks old, it is likely to grow up fearful.

Unfortunately, the vaccines your puppy needs to fight disease will not be totally effective by this time. A compromise is to carry your puppy everywhere you go, but with giant breeds this might be a little difficult. The sooner your dog travels in cars, hears traffic noises, meets children and all the other things he'll have to contend with, the easier it will be for him to accept his environment.

Puppy training has advanced tremendously in recent years. Reward-based training methods are now becoming more popular than the old school of choke chains and punishment. Training can start very early. Puppy socialization groups are the first step and they are very enjoyable for dogs and owners alike. Puppies mix with dogs of different breeds and learn vital communication skills. The classes are particularly useful for making sure small or big dogs learn how to play safely with other breeds. Your vet will often know where your nearest puppy socialization group meets.

Housetraining myths and methods

Anyone who has ever come home to a puddle and scolded their pup will be shocked to hear dogs can only link their actions with your punishment if you act within two seconds of their misdeed.

That guilty look we have always thought meant they knew they'd done wrong is simply their reaction to you coming home and being upset. In the past hour they probably did hundreds of things apart from that puddle — how would they be able to reason which of their actions was the one that offends? Guilt is a human emotion that dogs are lucky not to share. He looks sheepish because when there's mess in the room, you start acting oddly — he thinks your aggression is unprovoked.

Rubbing your dog's nose in the 'accident' may relieve *your* frustration — but it won't cure the problem.

Puppies that have lived in a kennel environment for too long might be more difficult to housetrain than those brought up in a house. Dogs will naturally keep their den clean, but this trait may be damaged if you keep a dog in an area too small to allow them to keep their living area free of mess. Small dogs are often more difficult to housetrain than big dogs because of the relative differences in their perception of distance. For example a Yorkie will think the next room is a long way away from his bed.

Housetraining is easiest if you do not allow the dog to develop bad habits like fouling inside the house. Instead, make sure you take your dog into the garden at regular intervals. If you see your puppy about

to squat in the house, lift him up and quickly take him outside. When he goes where you want him to, give lots of praise and even a tit-bit. If you can't watch very closely, try using an indoor kennel containing his bedding — which he is unlikely to foul. Make sure you take the puppy into the garden very regularly and give him lots of praise when he gets it right.

The importance of training

The most common cause of death for a young dog is being put to sleep for bad behaviour. If this happens to your dog you will have to live with the guilt of knowing you failed to teach the dog to behave properly. Bad behaviour in a puppy may be the cause of amusement. Everyone loves a little pup to jump up, to bark with excitement and chew slippers. Unfortunately, your dog doesn't understand why you're displeased six months later when he puts his paws on your shoulders.

Encourage the behaviour you want to live with from the start, it's much easier.

For example, if your puppy play bites, let him know it really hurts — even if it doesn't. A loud 'YeOwww' from you will teach him humans are very sensitive. If you ignore him for the next five minutes and look upset, he'll soon realize if he closes his jaws on human flesh it ends the game. This lesson needs to be learned early — before those puppy needle teeth are replaced with enormous fangs.

Body talk

Dogs really do pick up on body language — so you have to be convincing. A 'good dog' through gritted teeth is easily translated by your dog to mean 'bad dog'. They don't understand the words you say — they read your intonation and body language — which is much more revealing. Practise showing your emotions to your dog. Giggle, laugh, dance when you're pleased with him. If he makes you cross, have a temper tantrum and take it out on a cushion. You should never need to raise a hand to your dog in anger, violence breeds violence. Just communicate that you are the boss and you are displeased.

16

Caring for your dog

Selecting a vet

Choosing a vet is best done on personal recommendation. Selecting the cheapest is not always a good idea. Often the less expensive surgeries will not have the money to invest in modern equipment and should your dog need complicated care, you may find the facilities are not available. Dog veterinary care is now so advanced that often the only restriction on treating an illness or injury is financial. Many people solve the worry of unexpected bills by taking out pet health insurance.

The vet you choose should be easy to talk to and good with your dog. Consider rejecting surgeries that insist on your dog going up on a table for examination. This will be for the benefit of the vet's back — many dogs are upset by being on a high table and you want to reduce stress if your dog is unwell. Some vets spend a fortune on uniforms, nice lighting and pot plants. See these as window-dressing for your benefit.

Vet's waiting rooms are often full of miserable dogs shaking with fear. This need not be the case. Introduce your dog to the vet and make it a good experience. Ask him to give your pup a tasty treat and a good pat — even if he has come in for an injection. Also ask the vet nurses to do the same every time you visit. That way your dog will associate the experience with happy events and will be a lot less traumatized.

Regular healthcare

You should be a regular visitor to your vet. Your first few visits will be for the all-important vaccinations against highly contagious diseases. During those visits you should discuss worming and start a regular programme. Dogs should be wormed several times a year for the benefit of their health. A lot of publicity has been given to the risk to humans from dog worms. This has been greatly exaggerated and sensationalized. There is a much greater risk from cat and fox mess, but it is still in everyone's interests to keep up to date with worming.

Your veterinary surgery is the best place to buy worming tablets as they will be able to weigh your dog and prescribe the correct dosage. It is also the place to go if your dog has a problem with fleas or other parasites. If he does pick up some unwelcome visitors, you have to treat your house as well as him. There are special sprays you can buy that should be used on your carpets, the dog's bedding and anywhere else the dog likes to sit.

There are a number of products you can use to deter parasites from leaping on your dog in the first place. There are sprays, collars, wipes and long-lasting capsules that can be poured onto the back of your dog's neck. Some people put their faith in natural remedies such as garlic.

Grooming

Whatever type of dog you choose, grooming will be important. There is a theory that short-coated dogs tend to be less friendly than hairier types because they are less used to being groomed by their owners.

Grooming is an easy way to show your dog who is in charge. It gets him used to being touched. It should be an enjoyable experience and if you start when the dog is very young, the dog will learn to lie still and relax. Apart from brushing and combing there are other important grooming rituals. If your dog doesn't get enough exercise on hard surfaces, its claws can grow very long causing the dog discomfort.

The nails will need regular clipping. Ask the breeder, your vet or a dog groomer to show you how to do this. It is important you get the right equipment for the strength of your dog's nails and that you avoid cutting in to the quick as this will cause a great deal of pain and bleeding.

If your dog needs a bath, you should be careful to use a dog shampoo. Human shampoos tend to contain chemicals which can irritate the dog's skin. Make sure you rinse and dry your dog well afterwards. A useful tip to make your dog shake himself dry is to give him a very gentle tickle just inside the ear (be very gentle). If you start early it is possible to train your dog to accept a hairdryer.

If your dog starts to drag its bottom along the floor some people say it is a sign of worms — this is unlikely. It usually means the dog's anal glands need emptying. Ask the vet to show you how to do this as it's something you can do at home.

Feeding

There is a huge variety of different foods available. Try to feed your puppy on the same diet he was given before you got him, as a drastic change will probably upset his stomach. If you do want to change the food, do it very gradually. Foods can be complete or complimentary

— either containing everything your dog needs or requiring another food to be added. If you are giving your dog a complete food, be careful not to overdo the vitamins and minerals. For example, too much calcium and vitamin D can be as damaging as too little — bones can crumble and bone diseases can occur. If your puppy does get an upset stomach, contact your vet for advice immediately.

As well as trying to keep your pup's food consistent, why not do the same with his water? Take a container with you and ask the breeder to fill it up. Use bottled still mineral water for the first few days, and then wean your dog onto your own tap water. When your pup has finished growing, make sure you keep a constant eye on his weight. Obesity is a major health problem for dogs. It can aggravate arthritis and be a trigger for cancers, too.

Your vet can help put your dog on low-calorie dog food if cutting down proves traumatic.

Selecting boarding kennels

From time to time you may need to leave your dog in kennels. Rather than put your dog in kennels for two weeks while you go on holiday with a heavy heart, give him a couple of trial runs. Book your dog in for a day, or just an afternoon if they'll let you. Then leave him for a weekend. He'll soon realize you come back and it's not so bad. When you go away for a longer period, he won't fret and neither will you. When choosing kennels, personal recommendation is always a good starting point. Visit a couple of kennels, and talk to the kennel staff. Ask as many questions as you like and check out the security of the runs first hand.

If you cannot imagine leaving your dog in kennels, you might consider paying a trained carer to come into your home to look after your pet. There are now several agencies offering this service and they can often look after other pets, including horses! It can be a little expensive, but there is the added advantage of your house being occupied while you're away.

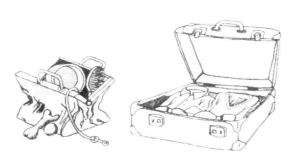

Tail docking

Nearly 50 breeds of dog usually have their tails docked. If you do not want this to happen to the puppy you buy, you will have to approach the breeder before the litter is born and try to get agreement that your puppy will not be docked. The operation normally takes place, without anaesthetic, when the puppy is only a few days old.

Identification methods

Accidents can happen and if your dog gets lost you will want to be sure he will be returned to you. There are several methods of identification to consider. The most simple is the engraved tag on your dog's collar. This is instantly visual and should be used even if you also opt for one of the more sophisticated methods. Wearing a collar and dog tag is required by British law.

Tattooing is popular in some circles as it is a permanent marker which would hopefully deter someone from selling the dog to a laboratory for vivisection. Micro chipping is becoming more and more available. A small bead is injected into the dog's neck and it stores information which can be read by a scanner. The effectiveness of this method is limited by the number of people who own and use the scanners.

Bedding

There are lots of different beds on the market: bean beds, rigid plastic bowl-types, little hammocks, orthopaedic foam mattresses and even heated blankets for the most sensitive dogs.

For the early weeks a cardboard box is usually completely adequate and should the puppy chew, there are hundreds of replacements at your local supermarket.

Crates (portable metal cages) are becoming increasingly popular. It's easy to see the cage as a prison, but most dogs love the security and will choose to sleep inside even when the door is wide open.

Crates are useful for housetraining and they can be a life-saver if used in the car. Many serious accidents result from the tail gate flying open and some very frightened dogs heading off into the traffic.

Dogs, Cats and Children

Introducing dogs to cats

Dogs and cats don't have to be enemies. It just takes a bit of effort and forethought to ensure 'purr-fect' harmony. Cats who are not afraid of dogs will have few problems. If a cat is frightened and runs off, it triggers the dog's natural instinct for chase. If you are going to get a cat, try to find one reared in a doggie environment or at least try to get it while very young. A cat will normally become the pack leader, but until the order of your household is established make sure the cat always has high-level escape routes available should it feel the need to get away. A secure crate can also prove useful. It can protect the cat while the dog satisfies its curiosity.

Children and dogs

There are some rules children need to learn if they are to get along with dogs. An organization called Prevent-a-Bite gives the following guidelines:

- Never bother a dog when he is feeding.

- Don't tease your dog — his ears aren't hankies.

- If chased by a dog while cycling, get off, place the bike between you and the dog, and look away.

- Avoid packs of dogs. If confronted, don't run away or scream.

- Do not disturb a sleeping dog.

- If meeting a new dog, pat him on the side of the head, under the chin or chest. Never place your head above a dog's — crouch down and approach on his level.

- Ask the owner if it's okay to pat his dog. If it is, allow the dog to sniff your knuckles.

- Don't pat dogs in cars — it's a space they consider well worth defending.

- Don't try to separate dogs which are fighting — go for help.

- Never approach a dog that is tied up.

Preparing for a baby

Many dogs looking for a new home are doing so because the owner has had a baby and didn't prepare the dog for the new arrival. Many dogs don't get a second chance and they have a one-way trip to the vet. Press reports make mothers-to-be very nervous about keeping their dog. However, with careful planning, a new baby needn't mean a painful goodbye to your dog. Successful mother and multiple dog owner Liz Jay has formulated this checklist for expectant mothers:

- 'De-spoil' your dog — move his bed out of the bedroom.

- Go to obedience classes — when pushing a pram, you don't want a dog pulling on the lead.

- Get a good dogsitter and encourage your dog to be less dependent on you.

- If your dog has a long coat, consider asking the grooming parlour to take over — perhaps they collect?

- Keep worming and de-fleaing very regular.

- Banish bones to the garden.

- When you come home, pass baby to grandma and greet your dog.

- Let the dog sniff the baby and satisfy his curiosity.

- Don't show alarm when your baby cries — it will upset the dog!

- Always make time to show your dog you still care about him.

If you really can't cope

Sadly, some people decide they just can't cope with a young family and a dog. Before you make any decisions you might regret — pack the dog off to boarding kennels for a couple of weeks and see if getting rid of the dog is really the key to family harmony. If you still decide to let him go, contact the breeder first, if you have chosen a responsible one he will help find a new home.

How to be top dog

Dogs are pack animals and they feel much happier knowing who their leader is. Unfortunately they are not democrats — if you're not perceived to be the boss, they'll quickly become dictators and make your life a misery.

Being in charge doesn't mean being aggressive. There are lots of simple signals you can give that command respect — you just have to see the world through dog eyes.

In dog psychology the top dog always eats first. So, before you put your dog's bowl to the floor, eat your own dinner or at least be seen to enjoy a chocolate biscuit or a piece of toast.

When you are eating never let those big brown eyes get to you. If you share what you're eating, you're telling the dog you are subordinate to it. Simple things like walking through doors can reveal a lot about the pecking order. He who goes first is number one, so always make sure it's you!

If your dog is getting a bit power-crazed there are some steps you can take to regain control.

Allowing your dog to sleep in the bedroom is seen as the ultimate privilege — it's the centre of power. Just by moving your dog into the kitchen you will have gained his respect.

Whenever your dog is lying or standing in your way — make him get up and move, don't step over him. Making him give way to your wishes is a way of reinforcing your position.

If you play a game of tug of war — make sure you win. To your dog it's much more than a game.

If your dog is over-dominant or you are having any other behaviour problems and you need help, talk to your vet. He or she may refer you to a member of the Association of Pet Behaviour Counsellors.

How to be your postman's friend

Every year, thousands of postmen, milkmen and refuse collectors are bitten by dogs. Make sure your dog doesn't do this by spending a little time teaching him these people are his friends.

The postman-phobia often results from the dog believing the postman is frightened off every morning by his warning bark. How is the dog to understand that this stranger didn't want to enter the house? He just knows that when he barks he goes away. It irritates the dog that the postman doesn't learn the lesson to stay away so his barking becomes more indignant. Every day this pattern is repeated. As the dog's confidence grows the dog perceives the postman as a very cowardly person indeed. So much so that even the most timid dog will chance a bite if he meets him in the flesh. The refuse collector can be much more unpopular. The dog believes he steals all that wonderfully smelly rubbish from his garden.

Before this vicious circle begins you need to enlist the help of those people who regularly visit the house. If the postman can be persuaded to ring the bell instead of posting the letters through the box, you can have an early face-to-face meeting. If the postman can produce some tasty treats from his pocket and then occasionally post a couple through the letter box with your letters, your dog will be his friend for life.

Hereditary health problems

Just as in human medicine, there are hundreds of hereditary canine conditions. Brief mention has been made throughout this book of the most common. The best person to advise you is your vet. You can limit the chances of your puppy developing problems by only buying from a caring, responsible breeder who has tested his stock before breeding.

Hip dysplasia is prevalent in many large or heavy breeds and it is sometimes operable, but expensive. There are tests that responsible breeders can ask vets to perform which grade the hips in degrees of normality. The figure given is known as 'the score' and roughly speaking the smaller the number the better. The object is to find a mate that compliments in every respect, but also has an even better hip score. To buy a dog bred from untested stock is like playing Russian roulette. The following list shows the ten best and worst breeds for hip dysplasia. It would be more unwise to buy a dog from the worst list without thoroughly researching hip dysplasia.

Breeds with best hips

 1 Irish Wolfhound
 2 Smooth Collie
 3 Siberian Husky
 4 Saluki
 5 Dalmatian
 6 German Short-haired Pointer
 7 Flat-coated Retriever
 8 Irish Red & White Setter
 9 Afghan Hound
10 Rhodesian Ridgeback

Breeds with worst hips

 1 Clumber Spaniel
 2 Otterhound
 3 Sussex Spaniel
 4 Newfoundland
 5 Schnauzer
 6 Bullmastiff
 7 Gordon Setter
 8 Briard
 9 Hungarian Puli
10 St Bernard

Other hereditary conditions

Eye problems are probably the next most common hereditary conditions. Again there are tests which the parent dogs should take. Eye problems can come in many forms. For some conditions the dogs need to be tested regularly as a problem can arise suddenly. For others there will be a once and forever test.

Some problems are breed-specific and need in-depth research. Unfortunately, osteochondritis (OCD), which afflicts many breeds, does not have an official testing system in Britain as yet. Some breeders dispute that it is a hereditary condition. Elsewhere in Europe, breeders have begun to eradicate this painful affliction which can affect the elbow, shoulder, stifle and hock joints of young dogs.

Responsible ownership

A recent newspaper survey revealed the most unpopular thing in Britain to be dog dirt — beating violent crime and unemployment by a mile.

Owners who continue to allow their dogs to foul in public areas put everyone's right to exercise their dogs off lead at risk. Scooping the poop is easy, just put your hand inside a strong plastic bag — grab the offending mess, turn the bag inside out, knot it and dispose in a dog bin. Never go anywhere without a plastic bag in your pocket — or better still train your dog to go at home.

Hobbies for your dog

Does your dog like chase games? Perhaps you find his recall unreliable and so can't give him the free exercise you'd like? Racing may be the sport for your dog. All breeds of dogs can go along to special race meetings and have a good gallop. It's excellent fun for all concerned and a great way of giving your dog a lot of exercise.

Does your dog love meeting people? Have you considered registering him as a hospital visitor? It's a very rewarding pastime.

Agility and Flyball are fast and furious ways for an obedient dog to let off steam. Ask the Kennel Club to put you in touch with your nearest training club.

How old is your dog?

We all know the one dog year equals seven formula, but there is a much more accurate measure as shown in the box chart below.*

CANINE		HUMAN	CANINE		HUMAN
3 months	–	5 years	8 years	–	48 years
6 months	–	10 years	9 years	–	52 years
1 year	–	15 years	10 years	–	56 years
2 years	–	24 years	12 years	–	64 years
3 years	–	28 years	14 years	–	72 years
4 years	–	32 years	16 years	–	81 years
5 years	–	36 years	18 years	–	91 years
6 years	–	40 years	20 years	–	101 years
7 years	–	44 years	21 years	–	106 years

Life-expectancy varies from breed to breed. This chart would be for a breed with an average life-expectancy of 14 years. Smaller breeds tend to live longer and giant breeds seem to have very short life-spans — even though they have a lengthy adolescence.

Breed	Average life-expectancy	Age at maturity
Irish Wolfhound	8 years	2.5 years
Great Dane	9 years	2.5 years
Rottweiler	11 years	2.5 years
Old English Sheepdog	10.5 years	2 years
Boxer	12 years	3 years
German Shepherd	10 years	3 years
Weimaraner	11 years	3 years
Bearded Collie	14 years	2 years
Bulldog	9 years	2 years
Dachshund (Standard)	14.5 years	10–12 mths
Cavalier King Charles Spaniel	13 years	14–16 mths
Yorkshire Terrier	14.5 years	2.5 years

* First published in *Dogs Today* magazine. If you would like a sample copy of the magazine please write to: Dogs Today, 6 Station Parade, Sunningdale, Berkshire, SL5 0EP.

CHIHUAHUA
SMOOTH & LONG COATED

1–2·75kg

The smallest breed of dog in the world. Widely believed to have originated in Mexico, but some evidence suggests a Mediterranean birthplace. Known as pocket-dogs in Malta.

A big dog in a small body. Agile, courageous and quite fiery. Intelligent companions who thrive on love. Sometimes shy and suspicious of strangers. Quite enthusiastic mousers. Good with cats and other pets.

Two coat types — long and smooth. Long coats have soft feathering on the ears, legs, a pronounced ruff around the neck and a glamorous plumed tail. Compact with well-sprung ribs and a deep brisket. Any colour permitted. Should move with a brisk positive action. Eyes round but never protruding.

Wonderful friends for elderly people. They require little food or exercise and give a convincing warning bark. Too fragile for young children or hectic households.

20–28cm

Some argue that a Roman statue from the second century AD features the breed. Paintings from the 13th century onwards display more certain evidence. The breed spread from Central Europe to become a royal favourite in many countries.

Astonishing levels of intelligence are recorded in this breed. Surprisingly resilient and hardy types who love their owners with a passion and will defend them from intruders with disproportionate tenacity. Playful and always keen to learn.

The breed has two types — the Papillon with erect butterfly-type ears and the drop-eared Phalène (French for moth). They should be predominantly white with patches of any other colour permissible, (except in the UK where liver is frowned on). A dainty but sound dog with a silky coat.

Long-living, often reaching late teens. Splendid coat needs regular attention, although it keeps fairly clean. Enjoys long walks but will adapt to fit in. Excellent housedog for many.

POMERANIAN

1·8–2·05kg

Named after Pomerania in the Baltics where some early dogs sent to England originated. Breed used to be much larger — as shown in Gainsborough's portrait of Mrs Robinson. Owners include Queen Victoria, Mozart and Napoleon's Josephine.

Busy little dogs that can be a bit yappy if owners let them. They adore attention and will show off at every opportunity. Fearless with bigger dogs and highly indignant if challenged. Some can be short-tempered: seek out parents of sweet nature.

The smallest spitz breed. Foxy intent expression. Dark, slightly oval eyes which sparkle. A proud, almost arrogant head carriage. Self-important bustling movement. Many colours are possible. Double coat accounts for the way it stands off the body. A soft undercoat with an abundant harsher long outer coat.

The coat takes considerable work to keep in order — daily grooming a must. Happy with access to a small garden, but will cope with more exercise very well. Some hereditary problems.

YORKSHIRE TERRIER

Show weights to **3·1kg**, pets often larger

The larger pet Yorkies look more like the original breed than the tiny, delicate show specimens. Originally a tough, sturdy little terrier bred to catch rats in the Yorkshire mines. Breeders rapidly turned the Yorkie into a fashion accessory.

The fiery terrier temperament often surfaces. A brave guard dog which will usually attempt to catch a rabbit or rodent. Intelligent, affectionate pets which put up with pampering but appreciate a good walk and being treated like real dogs.

The show specimens and pet types vary greatly. Show points include a rich tan and steel-blue, long, silky coat. Many pet Yorkies have black markings that never turn blue. The little red bow does have a practical use, preventing irritation to the eyes. Tail is often docked. Eyes should not protrude.

Very popular dog with flat owners because of the small size. Coat needs regular attention. Some people choose to have the coat trimmed at a grooming parlour to make it more manageable.

Dachshund is German for "badger dog". Probably because "hund" was incorrectly translated they are classified as hounds rather than terriers. Egyptian wall-paintings and Mexican carvings show similar dogs, but German origin is claimed.

A hunting dog, miniaturized by selective breeding and introduction of Pinscher, Papillon and Schnauzer bloodlines in the early 20th century. Intelligent, some would say crafty and a little difficult to master. Long-haired more independent.

Bold, defiant head carriage. Over-long backs can be a recipe for spinal problems. Shoulder height should be half the length of body. Three varieties: smooths have dense short coats, longs have silky featherings and wires have short, straight, harsh coats. All colours allowed, but white markings usually undesirable.

Affectionate, close companion with a dry sense of humour. Probably not ideal for young families, happier to be the centre of attention. Long coats need a regular grooming regime.

GRIFFON BRUXELLOIS

2·25—5kg

In the late 19th century, the Griffon Bruxellois was born from a mixture of Affenpinscher, Belgian street dog and Pug blood. Probably used as vermin-controllers in the stables belonging to Brussels' hansom cabs, they would often ride beside the driver.

A cheeky little dog with great intelligence. Very trainable and full of fun. Due to its earlier employment as a ratter, has a terrier-type disposition. A very entertaining companion, always alert and watchful.

Usually docked. Often described as monkey-like. Stocky dogs with large heads. Prominent upturned chins give a petulant look. Wide distance between small ears. Two coat types — roughs are Griffon Bruxellois and the smooths Petit Brabançon. Red, black or rich tan and black. Frosting on mature smooths allowed.

Not as delicate as you might imagine. The rough coats need stripping a couple of times a year and daily grooming. Smooths only need a polish. Whiskers and eye area need careful washing.

ITALIAN GREYHOUND

2·75—4·5kg

The Romans are believed to have taken the breed from Egypt to the Mediterranean region in the 6th century BC. In more recent centuries, the breed became very popular in European courts. Famous owners include Queen Victoria and Frederick the Great.

Depending on how you raise this breed, it can be a sensitive little soul, easily frightened, or a happy, outgoing dog that is rarely fearful. Intelligent, relishing companionship. Can put on a tremendous burst of speed in pursuit of a rabbit.

A dog which always looks elegant, whatever the activity. The gait is one of the most attractive features of the breed. The high-stepping action is similar to that of a hackney pony. All shades of black, fawn, red, cream, blue with or without broken white. Coat thin and glossy like satin.

They crave cosiness. If you don't like jackets for dogs, don't buy this breed! Free from all doggy smells, seldom moulting. Enjoy exercise, can make do with a reasonable sized garden.

Up to **5.5kg**

Punishment for stealing a "lion dog" from the Chinese court was often death. In 1860, British and US troops marched on the Imperial palace. Five dogs came back with them. Conventional imports followed. The breed is now virtually extinct in China.

Brave, reputed to have the courage of a lion. Very determined and, should they get the upper hand, a tendency to be a little cranky. A lot of self-esteem, dignity and considerable intelligence. Occasionally stubborn.

Massive broad skull, flat and wide between the ears. Big, dark round eyes. Should weigh unexpectedly heavy when picked up. The breed moves with a definite rolling gait as it is much heavier in front than behind. Abundant mane with long feathering on the ears, legs and tail. All colours apart from albino and liver.

Can have breathing difficulties and eye problems. Needs quite a lot of grooming and careful cleaning of the face and eye area particularly. Little exercise required.

These two breeds were only separated in 1965 and to most eyes they only differ in ear carriage. As you might expect, these dogs are from East Anglia. Irish, Border and Cairn Terriers are believed to feature in the breed's ancestry.

Always on the go, hunting for rabbits and rats. Happy, intelligent dogs which can adapt well to family life. Seldom start a fight, but will give as good as they get! Always keen to please and will provide good notice of intruders.

Small, low and compact. A misleading innocent expression, particularly in the drop-eared Norfolk. All shades of red, red wheaten, black and tan or grizzle accepted. White markings undesirable. Hard, wiry coat, longer on the shoulders. Distinctive eyebrows and whiskers. Usually docked.

A good family pet, but availability may be a problem. Children should be firmly instructed not to tease. Has a lot of energy — needs at least a couple of trips to the park every day.

Thought to have been introduced to the Canary Islands by Spaniards. In the 14th century, Italian sailors re-discovered the breed and brought it back to Europe. It quickly became popular with the nobility. Less exclusive by late 19th century.

Friendly, outgoing, intelligent dog. Adores companionship but has plenty of dignity and self-possession. The word Bichon is French for lap dog. Bred as a pet for generations.

Very Poodle-like coat, but the rounded trim gives the breed a teddy bear-like appearance. Black buttons for eyes. Should move with dignity and style. Body is slightly longer than high. There should be a slight rise in the back-line over the loin. White, but cream and apricot markings acceptable up to 18 months old.

Needs daily grooming, frequent bathing and clipping. Bred to be a pet, so temperament makes him good for most households. Needs regular exercise. Can have weeping eye problems.

CAIRN TERRIER

28–31cm

Fox, badger and otter in the Highlands of Scotland came to hate the Cairn Terrier — or the short-haired Skye as it was once called. Because of the nature of their work, they had to be very agile and lighter-coloured dogs were preferred.

Although the breed will still go after a rabbit if it gets the chance, it also enjoys being a pet providing it gets plenty of exercise and stimulation. Would rather be with you than left at home and can be sulky if things don't go its way.

Strong and compact, looks workmanlike. Eyes wide apart and slightly sunken. Shaggy eyebrows. Very free-flowing movement. Front feet larger than hind feet. Tail gaily carried. Weatherproof coat. Cream, wheaten, red, grey or nearly black. Brindle accepted. Not solid black, white or black and tan.

Lives happily in a small flat, so long as gets lots of walks. Needs grooming two or three times a week. Jealousy shouldn't be tolerated; must respect children as pack leaders, too.

Once claimed as a Dutch dog, other theories include Russian origins, Mastiff relations or even some Chinese connection. The name is thought to come from the Latin "pugnus", meaning closed fist, which is what the Pug's head is said to resemble.

An unusual character, intelligent and adaptable. Possessing great charm and self-esteem. Reliable and very expressive. Occasionally mischievous. Can tend towards gluttony. Sometimes sulky and aloof with strangers.

Massive solid round head. Short, blunt muzzle with obvious wrinkles. Very large eyes, thin soft ears. Bottom jaw slightly protruding, thick arched neck. Cobby body. High-set tail with a double twist highly desirable. Silver, apricot, fawn or black. Black moles on cheeks, black trace from head to tail.

Suffers in heat and in cold. Can have breathing problems, choose parents that breathe easily. Eyes can be weepy. Equally good family dog or lone companion. Little grooming or exercise.

MALTESE

Up to **25cm**

There is a dispute as to whether the breed originates from Malta or Melita in Sicily. Statues depicting a similar looking type of dog have been discovered in Egyptian tombs and it's possible the Romans brought the breed to England.

Thanks to a long partnership between this breed and Man, they have a very special temperament. Gentle, good with children and obedient. Very loving and intelligent and capable of learning many commands.

Very elegant when the coat is properly cared for. Silky, white, long hair. Dark, intelligent eyes. Long ears that are well-feathered, mingling with shoulder hair. Feathered tail carried over the body. Square in body with free movement. Pure white — slight lemon markings permissible.

A sweet-natured dog that is a perfect pet in many regards. However, the coat is a considerable undertaking — daily grooming at least. Needs minimal exercise; perfect for a flat.

The Westie seems to have originated from a variety of small working terriers popular in Scotland at the turn of the century, its forte being otter and fox control. In 1904, all the regional varieties merged under this breed heading.

Quite a wilful dog, full of character. Self-confident and sometimes quite cheeky. Is still interested in chasing the odd rabbit. Can be sharp with intruders, or guests he decides are unwelcome! A small dog with a big dog mentality.

Pure white apart from eyes, nose, paws and toe-nails, which should be black. Strongly built. Slightly domed skull, head thickly covered with hair. Jaws strong and level. Eyes set wide apart under heavy eyebrows. Small erect ears. Tail should never be docked. Double coated. Harsh outer, soft underneath.

Not as easy an option as a breed developed as a pet. Westies have inbuilt hunting instincts. Need good upbringing to keep them in line. Require trimming and regular brushing. Moderate exercise.

SHIH TZU

The breed name stems from the Chinese *Shih Tzu Kou* meaning lion dog. However, the breed probably goes back to Tibet where it was believed to be a prized holy dog in the 7th century AD. Shih Tzu and Pekingese were sometimes interbred in China.

Intelligent and companionable, this is a breed that can be happy in town or country. Very independent, but adaptable. Extremely affectionate and playful. Enjoys sharing its owner's life. Does not like being shut in the house alone all day.

Sturdy, fully coated with an arrogant look. Broad head, good width between the eyes. Full beard and whiskers. Hair grows upwards on the nose. Wide mouth with bottom teeth and jaw slightly protruding. Black nose. Length of body greater than height at the withers. All colours permissible. Long, dense hair.

The considerable grooming requirement is probably the only drawback of this breed. Be careful to avoid pinched nostrils. Check that parents have no trouble breathing.

One of four Tibetan breeds. The three smallest have a lot in common — the Tibetan Spaniel, Tibetan Terrier and Lhasa Apso. Both the Tibetan Terrier and the Lhasa probably descend from long-haired herding dogs of Asia.

Highly intelligent dogs. Although most breeds claim their dogs to be bright, the Lhasa has a strange all-knowing quality which surprises other dog owners. Fearless — can sometimes be too good a guard, defending the family from all visitors.

Hair traditionally falls over the eyes, but if you want to tie it back, visibility will be improved. Dark eyes, pendant ears. Under jaw slightly prominent. Strong well-arched neck. Longer length of back than height at shoulders. Golden, sandy, honey, dark grizzle, smoke, parti-colour, black, white or brown.

Good family dog or lone companion. The coat care commitment is quite a responsibility and if you don't like daily brushing, look elsewhere. Minimal exercise necessary.

SCOTTISH TERRIER

25·4—28cm

Once described as the Aberdeen Terrier and probably originating from the same pool of working terriers that spawned the Westie and Cairn Terrier. Used to hunt for badger, fox and vermin. First breed standard was drawn up in 1883.

Definitely one of the family. Known for stubbornness and independence of spirit which earns him great respect, but can be a little frustrating at times. Loyal and faithful, reserved, but courageous when provoked.

Long head for size of dog. Almond-shaped eyes, deeply set under eyebrows. Keen intelligent expression. Large nose. Neat erect ears set on top of skull. Well-rounded ribs, short muscular back. Level top-line, powerful hindquarters. Front feet slightly larger than back feet. Black, brindle or wheaten of any shade.

Coat needs attention — professional assistance sometimes required to keep him looking his best. Terrier temperament means you'll have to train him well. Needs considerable exercise.

Corgis have been kept in South Wales for hundreds of years by farmers for herding cattle and ponies. The Pembroke and Cardigan divide is ancient, although some interbreeding did occur. The breed is mentioned in the Domesday book.

The Pembroke is bolder than the Cardigan. Faithful companions which make excellent watchdogs. As their working instinct was to snap at the heels of the cattle, old habits die hard. Early training must stop this behaviour from being applied to humans.

Pembroke: Strong and sturdy. Foxy head. Medium-sized ears. Fairly long neck, medium length body. Short tail, preferably natural. Red, sable, fawn, black and tan with or without white markings. **Cardigan**: Long in proportion to height, fox-like brush, large ears, any colour with or without white markings.

Surprisingly big teeth! Must be well brought up — quite suspicious of strangers and a little sharp with friends, occasionally. Minimal grooming. Plenty of daily exercise.

CHINESE CRESTED

23–33cm

Extinct in China, these dogs have a mysterious history. Perhaps brought to Mexico by the Toltecs who used them as temple dogs. Some believe the Mandarins had them as pets. In some countries, they are called Chinese Crested Temple Dogs.

Happy gentle dogs. Very affectionate and intelligent. Very active — always on the go — some say scatty. Protective towards property. Unhappy if left alone. Hairless reputed to be more tolerant than the Powderpuff variety. Easy to train.

Hairless usually has a plume of hair on the head, hairy feet and tail — rather like a Shire horse. Powderpuff is covered in a soft veil of long coat. Both coat varieties come in racy or cobby types. Head should be smooth without excess wrinkles. Dark eyes. Any colour or combination of colours is permitted.

Hairless needs protecting from sun. Needs regular bathing and baby oil. The Powderpuff is the more natural form of the breed. Hairlessness is caused by a lethal gene.

JAPANESE SPITZ

Relatively new to the world outside Japan, where it appears to have been developed from other spitz breeds, possibly Finnish Spitz and Norwegian Buhund. The breed bears a striking resemblance to the Pomeranian, only built on much bigger lines.

A little standoffish with strangers. Affectionate and companionable with friends. As with all spitz breeds, tends to be rather outspoken if this habit isn't controlled early on. Bright and a touch arrogant. Alert and lively.

Medium-sized head, pointed muzzle. Dark eyes with black rims. Small erect ears not too far apart. Small, round cat-like feet. High-set tail curled over back. Light, nimble movement. Double coat. Outer straight and stand-off. Undercoat short, dense and soft. Noticeable mane. Pure white.

Spitz temperament is not best suited to young families. Calmer homes stand more chance of controlling these relentless chatterboxes. Daily grooming needed. Moderate exercise.

TINY DOGS

Japanese Chin

Australian Silky Terrier

Sealyham Terrier

Affenpinscher

Skye Terrier

TINY DOGS

Tibetan Spaniel

Miniature Pinscher

English Toy Terrier

Schipperke

Lancashire Heeler

BASSET HOUND
PETIT BASSET GRIFFON VENDEEN

33–38cm

First recorded mention is in France in the mid-16th century. Employed to go to ground in pursuit of badgers. Basset means dwarf in French. Some believe they started as dwarfed versions of long-legged hunting dogs retained for curiosity value.

These are dogs with their brains in their nose. Still hunting dogs at heart and when a scent takes their fancy, there is no stopping them. Need activity and lots of exercise. House-training might be slow work. Thinks things over before doing what you ask.

Huge dog with very short legs. The Basset has much more wrinkling of skin on the legs than the Petit Basset and much greater bone. The very long, low-set ears and slightly droopy lower lids showing serious eyes are a feature not shared with Petit Basset, which offers a less exaggerated hairy alternative.

Only understanding, patient owners who enjoy the outdoors should be attracted to the Basset. Even though he's short, he's got the appetite of an enormous dog. Training is hard work!

Close relative of the Dandie Dinmont and the Bedlington — which came first is open to speculation. Used to work alongside a hunt called the Border Foxhounds. Known in Westmoreland and Cumberland in the 19th century.

Happy to be a house dog or to have a hard day hunting. Should be friendly with other dogs as his job was to work alongside the Foxhounds. Needs early conditioning to make him a friend of cats and other small animals.

Otter-like head. Dark, keen eyes. Small V-shaped ears. Deep, fairly long body. Strong loins and racy hindquarters. Should be sound enough to be able to follow a horse. Harsh, dense coat with a close undercoat and thick skin. Red, wheaten, grizzle and tan or blue and tan.

Unlike many other terriers, the Border only needs occasional stripping. Can adapt well to life in a flat or the city, but still needs plenty of exercise. Fairly easy to house-train.

MINIATURE SCHNAUZER

From southern Germany. Three varieties — Giant, Standard and Miniature — the Standard dating back to the 15th century. Schnauzer means snout. The Miniature variety is thought to have been created by crossing with the Affenpinscher.

Fearless and all-knowing. Reliable and intelligent. Larger dogs used by the army during war-time as message carriers. Affectionate, obedient and good guards.

Sturdy, almost square. Keen expression. Prominent eyebrows. Powerful, blunt muzzle. Stubby moustache and whiskers. Black nose with wide nostrils. V-shaped ears set high. Round, cat-like feet. Harsh, wiry coat. Black, or black and silver or pepper and salt in even proportion. Tail set high — usually docked.

An ideal small companion dog. Needs lots of exercise and daily grooming and some professional attention from time to time to keep him looking at his best. Usually good with children.

Often imagined to be a British native — the Beagle's ancestors probably came to England with William the Conqueror. Two sizes developed. The nine-inch Pocket Beagle, used on hunts on foot, died out. Very popular with Queen Victoria.

Like the Basset, another breed with its brain in its nose. Amiable companion, a little slow to learn — not due to a lack of intelligence, more likely because he believes he knows best. Pack animals which enjoy canine companionship.

Slightly domed skull. Broad nose, preferably black. Dark brown, fairly large eyes set well apart. Long ears, rounded at the tip. Should nearly reach the end of the nose when brought forward. Moderately long tail set high. Any recognized hound colour, not liver. Tip of stern white.

If you can persevere with the training and enjoy frequent outdoor exercise, this is an easy-to-care-for family dog. Kinder to keep this breed with another as it is a pack animal.

BULLDOG

22·5–25kg

The Bulldog's ancestors were used for bull-baiting (outlawed in 1835). Their prominent bottom jaw enabled the dogs to hang on to the bull with a vice-like grip and still breathe. Used to look more like the present-day Staffordshire Bull Terrier.

Very individual characters. Incredibly obstinate, they have to want to please you — they need to be persuaded. Doesn't take kindly to being laughed at, but will laugh with you. Good with children and will protect those they love. Sweet-natured.

Low, broad. Head massive and large in proportion to the body. Muzzle blunt and turned upwards. Hindquarters lighter than front. Body short. Jaws broad and square. Six small front teeth in a straight line. Tail set low. Walks with short, quick steps on tip of toes. Variety of colours.

Can suffer from breathing problems, especially during hot weather. Few puppies can be born naturally as the heads are too big to pass through the birth canal. Consequently prices high.

The breed was developed in America from English Cocker Spaniel imports. The main changes occurred around 1920 when the dogs started showing more height at the shoulder, longer necks and a change in head type. Coat also increased.

The hunting instincts of the breed are deeply submerged and it would take considerable effort to re-awaken them. Enjoys the companionship of people and is very adaptable. Very biddable and easy to train.

Short back which slopes to tail. Height approximately equal to length. Eyebrows clearly defined. Eyes round. Intelligent, alert expression. Coordinated movement, smooth and effortless. Silky, flat or slightly wavy coat. Black or other solid colours, parti-coloured all with or without specific tan markings.

You have to be quite a grooming fanatic to keep this dog looking good. Eyes need regular cleaning. Enjoys lots of exercise. Good family dog.

SHETLAND SHEEPDOG

36–37cm

Known on the Scottish islands as Toonie dogs, toonie being a farm. Used for keeping the sheep, ponies and hens in order but also part of the family. Collie, Icelandic dogs and even a King Charles Spaniel are reputed to be in their background.

Clean, gentle little dogs. Keen and willing to please. Really enjoy companionship but tend to dislike the attention of strangers. Sensitive, quick to realize if you are displeased. With an early start, can become very obedient.

Abundant coat. Sweet expression. Blunt, wedge-shaped head, tapering gently. Nose, lips and eye rims black. Almond-shaped eyes. Small ears, semi-erect with tips falling forward. Slightly longer in body than height. Tail set low. Graceful movement. Sable, tricolour, blue merle, black and white or black and tan.

An easy dog to live with, even cleans its paws like a cat! Easy to train, can be a little yappy if you allow it. Enjoys moderate exercise but needs some careful grooming. Good family dog.

King Charles II's dogs appear in many paintings. When dog shows started, the breed began to change — flatter faces were popular. In the 1920s, a prize was offered for the dog most like the paintings and the Cavalier King Charles was established.

Sweet, gentle dogs who love family life. Very adaptable to the needs of children and older people. Friendly, outgoing, affectionate, easy to train and very intelligent. Constantly wagging tails. Good with cats.

Cavaliers are much more popular than the King Charles. He is bigger and less snub-nosed than his near relative. Graceful. Large dark eyes. Long, silky coat. Black and tan, ruby (solid chestnut red), Blenheim (chestnut and white), tricolour sometimes called the Prince Charles. Tail occasionally docked.

Some grooming needed. The sweetest, gentlest nature making the breed an obvious choice for many families, older people or anyone who wants an easy life! Check line for heart problems.

STAFFORDSHIRE BULL TERRIER
36–40cm

This Midlands blend of bull and terrier seems to involve the Bulldog and the Old English Black and Tan Terrier. The breed was originally used for bull and bear baiting and later dog fighting until these pursuits were outlawed.

Fearless and an excellent guard dog. Has the same stubborn streak as the Bulldog. Much nicer to people than to other dogs. Very affectionate with children, intelligent and excellent company. Seems tough but has a heart of gold.

Very pronounced cheek muscles, strong jaws. Short neck. Wide front, close coupled body. Tail should look like an old-fashioned pump handle! Smooth, short, close coat. Red, fawn, white, black or blue or any of these colours with white. Any shade of brindle, or brindle and white.

Strong dogs which need careful owners to train them well. Careful socializing needed so they can mix well with other dogs. Very affectionate with people. Not so good with cats!

Originally called the Bull and Terrier and used for bull baiting until the sport was outlawed. James Hinks of Birmingham used the White English Terrier in Bull and Terrier breeding and produced the all-white strain which became the Bull Terrier.

If you don't exercise his body and brain, he will wreck your home. Never encourage a Bull Terrier to fight — it's much better to keep his past dormant. You must master him early. Clown-like and affectionate, good with children. Obstinate.

You either love his looks or hate them. Strongly built — known as the gladiator of the canine race. Unique down-face egg-shaped head. Triangular black eyes, well-sunken with a piercing glint. Small, thin ears. Short, low-set tail. Thick at root tapering to a fine point. Jaunty movement.

Athletic dog that needs plenty of stimulation. You definitely can't leave him to his own devices or you won't have a home to come back to. Needs good early training. Not good with cats.

JAPANESE SHIBA INU

36·5–39·5cm

Used for hunting small game in central Japan. The breed has changed little since the 17th century. It can trace its roots to primitive times. Thought to have originated from dogs brought from the South Seas.

Bright, active, keen and alert. Courageous, strong and spirited. Docile and faithful. In Japan, the breed is a pet, guard dog and working or sporting dog. Infrequent barkers, they can make most undog-like noises. Akita temperament in a pint pot.

Small, sturdy dog. Very slightly longer than high. Head a blunt triangle viewed from above. Small oval eyes. Triangular ears inclining slightly forward. Cat-like feet. Tail set high. Hard straight outer coat, soft undercoat. Red, black, black and tan or brindle, white with red or grey tinge.

An exotic dog, quite cat-like in some respects. Clean and industrious. But he can be quite difficult as he can also tend towards the fox. Definitely a big dog in a small package.

COCKER SPANIEL

Popularly believed to have originated in Spain some time before
the 14th century. Some theories believe the breed was used to
flush game for hawks. In the early 19th century, the name
Cocker was used to describe a dog that was used on woodcock.

The term merry little Cocker still applies. The ever-wagging
stumpy tail is a constant reminder. Very active, playful nature.
His role as the ideal family pet has had a bit of a beating with
reports of some solid colours developing rage syndrome.

Bustling movement. Square muzzle. Dark brown eyes.
Intelligent, alert, gentle expression. Low-set ears level with eyes.
Fine ear leathers extending to the tip of the nose. Thickly
padded, cat-like feet. Flat, silky coat. Various colours. In self
colours no white except on chest. Usually docked.

Lots of exercise needed. Coat needs considerable attention. Easy
to train. Be careful with solid colours. Check no history of rage
syndrome in the line. Otherwise, a very good family pet.

SMALL DOGS

French Bulldog

Glen of Imaal Terrier

Bedlington Terrier

Lowchen

Dandie Dinmont Terrier

Boston Terrier

Norwegian Buhund

Tibetan Terrier

Standard Dachshunds

HUNGARIAN PULI

37—44cm

A thousand years ago, the central Asian Magyar tribes invaded the central Danube region. With them came the Puli. For many centuries, it has been used to herd sheep on the Hungarian plains. It has became popular as a police dog.

Devoted, loyal and highly intelligent. However, can sometimes be very stubborn. As with many sheepdogs, slightly aloof with strangers, preferring his own family. Very fond of dogs of his own kind. Easily house-broken.

Long hair over eyes like an umbrella. Square from the side. Small head, slightly domed skull. Lively expression. V-shaped ears not obvious even when alert. Red tongue, dark roof of mouth. Tail curled over rump. Short-stepping movement. Black, rusty black, white, shades of grey and apricot.

Fascinating breed, not suitable for the average owner. Coat takes considerable care. Cords need help when they start and should you wash them, drying takes days. Some eye problems.

CLUMBER SPANIEL

Believed to come from France and the result of a cross between the extinct Alpine spaniel and a Basset Hound. They were much prized for their work as beaters and retrievers and were famed for their quiet work. In much demand with royalty.

Big hearted dog which is willing, but rather slow. Gentle and genial companion enjoying work and the outdoor life. Quite dignified and more aloof than other spaniels. Never shows any aggressive tendencies.

Massive head. Dark amber eyes, slightly sunken and showing some haw. Large, vine-leaf-shaped ears hanging slightly forward. Strong jaw. Rolling gait caused by a long body with short legs. Thick, silky and straight coat. Legs and chest well-feathered. White with lemon or orange markings.

Needs plenty of exercise. The breed has a bad record of hip dysplasia so be careful to pick a breeder that tests their stock before breeding and is showing some improvement.

Obscure origins. They came to the fore in the 19th century as part of foxhound packs, chasing the fox when it went to earth. The term Fox Terrier used to cover a wide range of terriers. The Wire and Smooth varieties were first denoted in the 1870s.

Friendly and placid and always good tempered. Playful, cheeky and occasionally full of mischief. Always ready for a scrap with another dog and fearless enough to take on all comers. Good with children and a fun dog to have around.

Short-backed dog. Quick moving. Dark eyes full of intelligence. V-shaped ears of moderate thickness, dropping forward close to cheeks. White predominates with black, black and tan or tan markings. Brindle, red, liver or slate blue markings undesirable. Usually docked.

The fiery spirit makes this dog a nightmare to take to the park. The wire coat needs quite a lot of attention. Needs plenty of exercise. Rather difficult to train, but a lovable companion.

First records show the breed as coming from Russia, but the word *pud(d)eln* (to splash) is German. It was developed as a water gundog and the curly coat protected it from the elements. The Miniature and Toy varieties were bred down from the Standard.

Intelligent dogs with an enormous sense of fun. Friendly and good-tempered. Should respond well to training. Very good company — adaptable to most lifestyles. Like to show off. Quite sensitive and, as such, probably prefer a calm household.

It's hard to look past the show trims that are popular. Underneath is a very sensible looking dog. Almond-shaped eyes. Long ears, set low. Proportionately small feet. Coat very profuse, harsh texture. All solid colours. Whites and creams should have a black nose. Tail set rather high. Usually docked.

Consider this breed if you have allergies to dog hair. They don't moult. Some sufferers find them non-allergenic. Test the theory out before you buy! They do need clipping and lots of exercise.

PARSON JACK RUSSELL
THE UNRECOGNIZED JACK RUSSELL

Up to **36cm**

Started in the early 19th century by Rev. Jack Russell of Devon. A very keen hunter, he needed a dog to go after foxes which had gone underground. The Kennel Club have recognized the Parson Jack Russell, but many short-legged JRs still elude classification.

Cheeky little devils, responsible for more bites than most other breeds of dog. They need careful discipline. Excitable, cheerful, excellent guards and ready to chase anything. Full of intelligence and tenacity.

Show type is longer on the leg than the average Jack. Jack Russells have two coat types, rough and smooth. Usually predominantly white with black or black and tan markings. Unregistered Jacks have a wide variety of shapes and sizes, but hunting instincts seem to be the unifying factor.

A lot of people get a Jack Russell not realizing how difficult they are to master. Unless very experienced in dog training, not ideal for a young family. A good guard, when mastered.

A relatively modern breed having evolved in Britain over the
past hundred years probably by crossing Italian Greyhounds
with terriers. Other theories include liaisons between Pharaoh
Hounds and Maltese Rabbit Dogs brought over by the Romans.

Some would say the ideal pet. Loving, affectionate, clean in the
house, easy to train and relatively undemanding. Very gentle and
calm. Will chase hares, rabbits and rats with a tremendous turn
of speed. This instinct will take a lot of suppressing.

Elegant but muscular. Built for speed. Long lean head, wide
between oval eyes. Rose-shaped ears. Long muscular neck,
elegantly arched. Not too wide in front. Very deep chest with a
definite arch over the loin. No feathering on the tail. Movement
not to appear mincing. Any colour or combination.

This is a dog for all households. Loves to curl up near a warm
radiator and doze. Affectionate with all ages. Vegetarians may
find the squirrel-chasing a bit hard to handle.

SAMOYED

46–56cm

Breed used to inhabit the forests of central Asia with the people who called themselves Samoyedes. The dogs herded reindeer and guarded them from bears. They were members of the family, sleeping in their tents and sharing their food.

Loves human companionship, believing himself of equal status. Independent and forever appearing to smile. Intelligent but not overly obedient. Like all spitz dogs, he thinks about obeying commands and tends towards the outspoken.

Wedge-shaped head. Black lips that seem to smile. Almond-shaped eyes. Thick ears rounded at tips. Neck arched. Long flattish feet. Cat feet undesirable. Body well-covered with thick, soft undercoat with harsh weather-resistant hair through it. White, cream or biscuit markings. Silver tipped.

Needs lots of exercise and grooming. Can be very vocal. Needs owners who are very experienced and can understand the spitz temperament.

43–46cm

A Dutch peasants' farm and barge dog. The breed is named after the leader of the Dutch rebels who rose up against the ruling House of Orange (they had the Pug as their mascot). The Keeshond was the dog of the people and a symbol of resistance.

Mainly a one-man dog, but can adapt to take the whole family into his heart. Bold, alert and very strong guarding instincts. Intelligent and adaptable. Sensitive and even-tempered. Like all spitz, can be a bit noisy.

Wedge-shaped head. Dark muzzle, black nose. Almond-shaped obliquely set eyes. Black line extends from inner corner of eye to ear. High-set tail, curled over back — double curl preferred. Brisk, sharp movement. Harsh, stand-off coat. Mixture of grey and black. Undercoat of pale grey or cream.

Daily grooming required and plenty of exercise. Experienced dog owners only should undertake spitz breeds. Could be noisy. With careful upbringing makes a good companion.

MEDIUM-SIZED DOGS

Welsh Terrier

Manchester Terrier

Australian Cattle Dog

Irish Terrier

Field Spaniel

MEDIUM-SIZED DOGS

Elkhound

Portuguese Water Dog

Finnish Spitz

Schnauzer

ENGLISH SPRINGER SPANIEL

WELSH SPRINGER SPANIEL   English: **51cm**. Welsh: **46–48cm**

The English Springer is said to be the older spaniel. The Welsh would probably disagree. The breed claims to be mentioned in the Laws of Wales circa 1300. Possible links with the Brittany Spaniel cannot be ruled out.

Easy to train but difficult to find enough to occupy these active, intelligent dogs. They love Man but they have a tremendous bond with dogs of their own kind, too. Faithful and willing but a working dog first and foremost.

English: Almond-shaped eyes. Good length of ear, nicely feathered. Good strong neck. Higher on the leg than other land Spaniels. Tail usually docked. Liver and white, black and white or either of these colours with tan markings. **Welsh**: Lighter build than the English. Smaller ears, rich red and white colour.

You have to have lots of time and energy for these breeds. If you don't keep them busy they'll be miserable and will take your house apart. Both breeds need regular grooming.

Natives of Ireland claim the breed has been pure for several centuries. Sceptics believe the Bedlington, Dandie Dinmont and Irish terrier have all played their parts. Strangely, County Kerry has never claimed the breed as its own.

Sweet and loving to people but a real fiend with other dogs. Extremely argumentative with most other canines yet gentle with people and quite easy to train. Extrovert and very good guarding instincts.

Compact and powerful. Long, lean head. Strong jaw. Eyes as dark as possible, keen expression. V-shaped ears, carried forward. Free, powerful movement. Soft, silky plentiful coat. Any shade of blue. With or without black points. Dark colour allowed up to 18 months of age. Tail usually docked.

Coat needs a lot of attention and it can be difficult to give this dog enough exercise as he's likely to fight with every dog in the park. Probably not very good with other pets either.

IRISH WATER SPANIEL

51–58cm

Over a thousand years old. There were two strains from the south and the north of the country. Today breed takes after the southern type. Probably goes back to Poodle and Irish Setter blood and some say a Curly Coated Retriever may be involved.

Easy to train, highly intelligent. Enduring, versatile. Enjoys hard work. Loves water. Initially, rather aloof but as you get to know the breed they develop a wonderful sense of humour that is very rewarding. Biddable and loyal.

Smooth face, large nose. Almond-shaped eyes. Oval-shaped ears set low. Powerful, arched neck. Large round feet, hair between the toes. Short tail, thick at root and tapering to a fine point. Rolling movement. Tight crisp ringlets, free from woolliness with natural oils. Rich dark liver with purplish bloom.

Coat needs little brushing — try not to bathe as it removes the natural oils. This is a dog that enjoys his work — so it probably isn't fair to give him too domestic an existence.

POLISH LOWLAND SHEEPDOG

40–51cm

Also known as the Polski Owczarek Nizinny. A herding dog from Poland said to be the missing link between the long-coated herders and the corded dogs. The Polish Lowland has been linked with the Bearded Collie's heritage.

A friendly, intelligent dog making it a good family pet. Lively, but self-controlled. Perceptive with an excellent memory. Easy to train. Watchful, bright and always alert, A good watchdog. Hardy and even-tempered.

Penetrating gaze. Medium-sized heart-shaped ears. Strong muscular neck without dewlap. Rectangular body rather than square. Oval feet. Body covered with long dense hair of harsh texture. Soft undercoat. Long hair covers eyes. Any colour. Usually docked if not born without a tail.

Grooming and exercise provide a considerable commitment, but good family dogs if you can cope. Check out the line before buying and avoid hip dysplasia and any other hereditary defects.

SHAR PEI

46–51cm

The breed can be traced back to the Han dynasty over 2,000 years ago. A hunter of wild boar, it also doubled as a protector of livestock and guarder of homes. If bad at the job, it was eaten! Taxes became very high and the breed barely survived.

Calm, affectionate with people they like, but like many Oriental breeds, they possess an independent streak. Alert and dignified. They tend to be one-person dogs and fairly inhospitable to strangers.

The Chinese describe the breed as having a head like a pear-shaped melon, clamshell ears, butterfly nose, shrimp back, ironwire tail and water buffalo neck! Bluish black tongue preferred. Free movement. Short bristly harsh coat. No undercoat. Solid colours — black, red, fawn or cream.

Beware. A breed with serious design faults. Breeders are trying to make them less wrinkly, but that's really their attraction. Skin and eye problems are common. Can be fiery with other animals.

78

CHOW CHOW

Blue tongues are rare in dogs — but they're common in bears!
Name stems from the word Chaou meaning "dog of strength" or
Tchau, the word for an important trader. The smooth variety
comes from central and southern China.

Silent and aloof. Very strong minded. An excellent guard. Very
much a one-man dog. Like other Oriental breeds, has a mind of
its own and will not be forced into doing anything. He would die
for you, but not obey you.

Compact, short-coupled. Lion-like. Dignified. Flat skull. Dark,
almond-shaped eyes. Tongue, roof of mouth and gums black.
Deep chest. Cat-like feet. Short, stilted movement. Two coat
types, rough and smooth. Rough has profuse stand-off coat and
soft, woolly undercoat. Black, red, blue, fawn, cream or white.

Not an easy first-time dog. Breed has considerable eye problems.
Entropion common (eyelids turning in). Check the line for
problems. Coat needs attention.

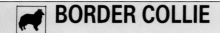

BORDER COLLIE

51cm

Like all working dogs, the history is vague. No paintings remain. The Collie has been man's partner for centuries. It has joined the pedigree ranks only recently. Hopefully, generations of breeding for brains will not be forgotten.

Quick-thinking dog that needs to be kept active or it will become neurotic and impossible to live with. Sensitive and sometimes quite sharp. In his working life he would have to be strong-willed to persuade the sheep who was in charge.

The show type of dog is quickly becoming more uniform. Pretty much anything goes for the farmer so long as the job gets done. Eyes wide apart, mild, keen alert expression. Ears can be erect or semi-erect. Coat can be rough or smooth and a wide variety of colours allowed, but white should never be dominant.

This breed doesn't easily make a good pet. It needs activity or it could snap. If it can make use of its natural talents, it will be a faithful friend. Check for hereditary eye problems.

The Polish Lowland looks similar to the Beardie. However, there are also close links with the Border Collie and the Old English, too. It could be that common ancestors are shared. Breed saved from dying out in the 1950s by Mrs Willison.

Huge sense of humour and clown-like qualities that keep you laughing. Affectionate and very gregarious with people and other animals. Natural herding ability still very strong. Loves human company. Very smart and sensitive.

Long bodied. Effortless movement. Able to go on all day. Sweet, gentle expression. Eyes and nose to match coat colour. Double coat. Outercoat harsh and not so bushy as to obscure the line of the dog. Soft undercoat. All shades of slate, brown, blue, fawn, tri-colour with or without white markings.

Coat can be a problem. It needs constant attention — they often bring a lot of the park home with them. Breed needs plenty of human contact and free-running exercise every day.

SIBERIAN HUSKY

51–60cm

Originates from Siberia. The huskies, owned by the nomadic Inuit, pulled sleds and herded reindeer for 3,000 years until traders took the breed to America early in the 20th century. The dogs were used by those searching for gold in Alaska.

A loyal family companion. He is not suspicious of strangers so will not guard your home. Gentle, affectionate, alert and outgoing. Eager disposition and very willing to learn — although teaching them not to pull on the lead is quite difficult!

Graceful action. Fox-like head. Almond-shaped eyes of any shade of blue or brown — one of each colour or parti-colours equally desirable. Triangular-shaped ears quite close together. Slightly longer in back length than height at the shoulder. Double coat, outer smooth-lying, soft undercoat. All colours.

No doggie smell with this breed. Coat doesn't take much grooming but inexperienced dog owners would struggle to understand this complex breed's temperament.

ROUGH COLLIE
SMOOTH COLLIE

The earliest ancestors of the breed probably arrived in Britain with the Romans, who often travelled with their dogs. Over the years, possible crosses with Borzoi, Deerhound and Newfoundland led to the creation of the breed as we know it.

Usually very clean animals. Occasionally highly strung, anxious to please and sometimes very shy of strangers. Good guard dogs and fairly easy to train. Probably still maintains some working ability but this is rarely tested.

Show people put great emphasis on the head. It should resemble a blunt wedge — smooth in outline from front or side. The illustration shows the sort of head many pet dogs have. Eyes almond shape set obliquely. Top third of ear tipping over (rare in pet Collies). Sable, white, tri-colour and blue merle.

Rough Collies need quite a lot of grooming — if this puts you off, go for the smooth — the coat's the only difference. Eye defects in this breed, so make sure your breeder tests for them.

GOLDEN RETRIEVER

51–61cm

In the mid-19th century, yellow wavy-coated dogs and Tweed water-spaniels were used in the border region of Scotland. Lord Tweedmouth combined dogs of both breeds to create the Golden Retriever, recognized by the Kennel Club in 1913.

This breed has the reputation of being the ideal family pet. However, the breed is quite different in the working and show worlds and you must choose whether you prefer the more active, athletic type or the calmer, heavier show specimens.

Balanced, powerful. Skull broad without coarseness. Dark brown eyes set wide apart. Black nose. Round, cat-like feet. Powerful driving movement, no sign of hackney movement. Flat or wavy coat with good feathering. Water-resistant undercoat. Any shade of gold or cream — neither red nor mahogany.

Needs plenty of exercise, eats quite a lot and needs regular grooming. Reputation as the perfect pet is being tarnished by indiscriminate breeding. Be careful in your choice of breeder.

LABRADOR RETRIEVER

54–57cm

Developed in the 19th century from Newfoundland water dogs. By the end of the century out-crosses with Flat-Coated and Curly-Coated Retrievers and Tweed Water Spaniels were needed. All Labs traced to Lord Malmesbury's dog Tramp.

Good-tempered, intelligent, strong will to please. Kind, gentle nature. Keen and biddable. Popular choices as assistance dogs. Good sense of smell combined with their trainability means they are excellent sniffer dogs.

Broad skull, intelligent eyes. Ears not too large, set far back and hanging close to head. Powerful neck. Deep chest with well-sprung ribs. Tail thick at the base tapering to the tip, densely coated giving an otter-like appearance. Short coat — hard to the touch. Black, yellow or chocolate.

Very popular pets. They need lots of exercise and careful attention to diet as they have a tendency to get fat. Make sure you buy from a breeder who tests for hereditary defects.

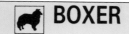

BOXER

54–64cm

Boxers were created in Germany at the end of the 19th century chiefly from the Bullenbeiszer and the Barenbeiszer, two ancient Mastiff varieties. Bulldog blood may also have been introduced. Became popular in Britain and America after World War II.

Alert and playful. Loves the companionship of people. Fearless, self-assured. Loyal to the family and suspicious of strangers. Affectionate and great potential to be obedient. Intelligent and full of character.

Noble and muscular. Lower jaw protruding, curving slightly upwards. Thick lips. Dark brown eyes. Ears wide apart. Round neck, clean cut and strong. As high at the shoulder as it is long in the body. Cat-like feet. Fawn or brindle colours, but white does occur. Tail usually docked.

Good companion — excellent family guard. Needs lots of exercise but minimal grooming. Very susceptible to cancer. White Boxers need careful checking for deafness and blindness.

OLD ENGLISH SHEEPDOG

56cm upwards

Originates, probably, from the Bearded Collie and imported breeds such as the Russian Owtcharka. First used to guard flocks against predators, then more favoured as a cattle drover. Docking tails may have started to exempt owners from tax.

Should be bold, faithful and trustworthy. Never nervous or aggressive, however, some lines do have these problems. Steady and sensible but very protective of his owners. Faithful and home-loving. Intelligent and often boisterous.

Large, square head. Big, black nose. Eyes can be dark or china blue. Small ears. Short back rising over the loin. Well-sprung ribs. Bear-like rolling movement. Profuse coat, shaggy and waterproof. Any shade of grey, grizzle or blue — with or without white markings. Tail usually docked.

Extensive grooming essential. On wet days, not for the house-proud. Breeders should test for hip dysplasia. Check parents are outgoing. Lots of exercise needed. Very loud, deep bark!

HUNGARIAN VIZSLA

54–64cm

Some claim they date back to 1000 AD, others maintain they're a result of cross breeding Weimaraners with various types of Pointer. The breed was certainly known in Hungary in the 18th century. Particularly good at tracking hare and deer.

Very active. Intelligent and, with correct training, obedient. Gentle, sensitive and affectionate. Bred to hunt and unlikely to be able to suppress this instinct. Loves swimming and having a reason to use his brain.

Lean head, tapering, square muzzle. Slightly oval eye of darker shade than coat. Low-set ears, rounded V-shape. Short, level back. Well-sprung ribs. Cat-like feet. Graceful, elegant movement. Short coat, greasy to the touch. Russet gold. White marks accepted but undesirable. Tail usually docked.

An outdoor dog that needs a lot to do to keep him occupied. Only suited to the active family that can get out into the country regularly. Low grooming requirement.

GERMAN SHORT-HAIRED POINTER

54–64cm

The result of crossing Spanish Pointers with Bloodhounds to produce a dog that would both point and trail by scent. In the 19th century, became less stocky and English Pointer blood was introduced to improve speed and scenting powers.

Gentle, affectionate and mainly kind and even-tempered. Very loyal, alert and keen to learn. Energetic and enthusiastic and in need of stimulation to keep him really happy. Natural hunting instinct probably difficult to suppress.

Clean-cut head. Powerful jaws. Soft, intelligent eyes. Broad ears, set high. Deep chest. Firm, short back — not arched. Round to spoon-shaped feet. Smooth gait. Short flat coat, coarse to the touch. Solid liver, black or either colour with white spots or ticking. Tail often docked.

Energetic dogs always eager to work. Good-natured companions. Providing they get enough exercise, and plenty to think about, they make good pets with little grooming requirement.

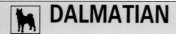

DALMATIAN

56–61cm

Much controversy surrounds the early history of the breed. Was it brought by Gypsies from northern India to Dalmatia? Or perhaps it was the Orient or even ancient Egypt or Greece? First noted as a carriage dog in the 18th century.

Lively, extrovert dog. Neither shy nor aggressive. Full of energy and enthusiasm. An excellent companion, if brought up to know the house rules. Particularly good with children. Loyal and devoted to the family.

Skull quite flat. Broad between ears. Long, powerful muzzle. Eyes set well apart. Intelligent expression. Ears set quite high. Deep chest. Tail reaching the hock — preferably spotted. Smooth, rhythmic movement. Short, hard, dense coat. Pure white background colour with dense black or liver spots.

This breed can be quite a handful as their enthusiasm for life can be a little draining if you don't have the same energy level! Sweet-natured. Needs lots of exercise. Check for deafness.

Probably originated in Weimar, Germany, by crossing Bloodhounds with local pointers and hunting dogs. Some suggest the breed was a mutation of the now-extinct black St Hubertus Brachen. Emerged in the early 19th century.

Fearless, friendly, obedient and protective — in the right hands. Strong-willed and very intelligent. Full of the will to hunt. Needs something to do that makes use of its mind and body. Has the potential to be sharper than the average gundog.

Grey nose. Eyes shades of amber or blue grey. Long ears. Strong jaws. Clean-cut neck. Deep chest, well-sprung ribs. Effortless movement. Short, sleek coat. Long-haired variety has feathered tail and limbs. Silver grey, but mouse or roe grey allowed. Metallic sheen. Tail usually docked.

Not a dog for a household with young children or older family members. This dog demands active companions who will treat him with a firm, fair hand and give him adequate stimulation.

AIREDALE TERRIER

56–61cm

Bred for otter hunting in Yorkshire by crossing the Welsh
Harrier, Otterhound and Old English Terrier. Originally called
the Bingley, Waterside or Warfedale Terrier, it became known
as the Airedale and was recognized by the Kennel Club in 1879.

A lively and fun-loving pet. Friendly and loyal and an excellent
guard. Can easily become unruly without fair but firm handling.
Outgoing and confident. Not particularly aggressive, but fearless
when provoked.

Largest terrier. Long, flat skull. Powerful jaws. Dark, small
eyes. V-shaped ears. Short back, well-sprung ribs. Deep chest.
Small round feet. Legs straight when moving giving brisk, free
movement. Hard, dense and wiry coat. Saddle, back of neck and
tail black or grizzle, rest tan. Tail often docked.

Coat needs careful attention — combing and hand stripping.
Requires lots of exercise and a sensible upbringing. Hunting
urges may lead him astray on country walks.

PHARAOH HOUND

54–64cm

One of the oldest breeds. Little changed in 5,000 years. Favourites of the Egyptian Pharaohs and depicted on their ornate tombs. Brought to Malta and Greece by traders. Known on the islands of Malta and Gozo as rabbit dogs.

Alert, intelligent, friendly, playful and affectionate. Hunters by sight and scent. Good companions who really need to be kept active if they are to remain happy. Quick and agile; retaining a keen hunting instinct that would be difficult to suppress.

Long skull, well-chiselled. Blunt wedge viewed in profile. Amber intelligent eyes. Erect ears. Broad at base, fine and large. Flesh-coloured nose. Lithe body. Well-padded paws. Whip-like tail carried high when in action. Free flowing movement. Short, glossy coat. Tan or rich tan with some white marking allowed.

Needs lots of free-running exercise to be happy. Enjoys companionship. Coat needs little attention. Not happy with a town life. Adaptable to most climates.

93

For many centuries, dogs of similar type herded and guarded flocks of sheep in Belgium. When the lands became enclosed and rail and road removed the need for droving, the breeders formalized the breed into four types to protect its future.

Intelligent and vigilant. Wary, though never timid, aggressive or nervous. Very strong guarding and herding instincts. Used as police, army and guard dogs in Europe. Tendency to be sharp in the wrong hands.

Groenendael (1): black, with or without small white markings. **Tervueren** (2): shades of red, fawn, grey with black overlay. Tip of each hair black. Black mask on face. Both have long coats with dense undercoat. **Malinois** (3): like the Tervueren but short-coated. **Laekenois** (4): wiry, dry hair.

If the breed is for you, select the coat-type that most suits your lifestyle as the dog underneath is much the same. They love the outdoors and need plenty of exercise.

Known in Britain as the Foreign Sheepdog and then Alsatian Wolf Dog to avoid anti-German feeling during war-time. Finally called the German Shepherd Dog. Originally used for herding, farm work and guarding.

Very intelligent and dependable given good, early training. Sensitive but never fearful or cringeing. Watchful and slightly suspicious of strangers. Quick to learn and devoted to his master. Independent thinker, but keen to please.

Almond-shaped eyes. Intelligent, self-assured expression. Length of back exceeds height at shoulders. Bushy tail. Flowing movement. Outer harsh coat, thick undercoat. Black with tan or grey markings, all-black, all-grey, or grey with brown markings. White and long-coated types unpopular with show breeders.

Not for the uncommitted. Given lots of interaction and training, a very rewarding friend. Enjoys long walks. Long-coated types need lots of grooming. Only buy from hip dysplasia-tested stock.

LARGE DOGS

Hamiltonstovare

Ibizan Hound

Chesapeake Bay Retriever

Bouvier des Flandres

Curly Coated Retriever

Large Munsterlander

German Wirehaired Pointer

Flat Coated Retriever

BERNESE MOUNTAIN DOG
58–70cm

In the late 1800s, the Swiss Mountain Dogs were split into four types, of which the Bernese was the most popular. Used for sheep and cattle droving, herding and guarding and as a draught dog, taking baskets of weaving to market.

Kind and devoted to the family. Good-natured, friendly and fearless. Aggressiveness not tolerated. Slow to mature. Affectionate, of superior intelligence and reputed to have a very good memory.

Flat skull. Dark brown, almond-shaped eyes. Ears set high, triangular shaped. Compact body. Broad chest. Firm, straight back. Round feet. Bushy tail. Soft, silky coat, long and slightly wavy. Jet black with reddish brown markings on cheeks, over eyes and on legs and chest. White on head, chest, paws and tail.

Devoted family pet, excellent with children. Breed has some problems with hip dysplasia and OCD. Be careful to buy only from tested stock. Needs regular free exercise and grooming.

ITALIAN SPINONE

Two thousand years old. Used by marshland hunters because of its excellent swimming abilities. Thick, wiry coat protects from freezing water and thickets. Thought to have originated in France from the French Pointer, the Porcelaine and the Barbet.

Intelligent, companionable and affectionate, adoring children and family life. Faithful and courageous. Very patient. Intrepid and untiring. Hardy and adaptable with good guarding instincts and a will to work.

Kind expression. Round eyes, deep yellow or ochre. Triangular ears. Strong, short neck. Height equal to length. Slight slope from withers to loin, rise from loin to croup. Dew claws on all feet. Thick, wiry coat. Leathery skin. White with or without orange or brown markings. Tail often docked.

In right hands, wonderful pets. Need lots of companionship. Good with children. Require free-running exercise, some grooming. Check lines for hip dysplasia and OCD.

ROTTWEILER

58–69cm

First noted in the Middle Ages as hunters of boar. Later, they were used as cattle dogs. Butchers and cattle dealers also used the breed as a draught dog to pull their small carts. Then became popular as a police dog.

Bold and courageous. Self-assured and fearless. Never nervous, aggressive or vicious. Courageous, easily trained with natural guarding instincts. Highly intelligent, requiring sensible upbringing and early socialization.

Almond-shaped eyes, dark brown. Pendant ears. Strong, arched neck. Broad, deep chest. Straight back, not too long. Gait should give impression of strength and endurance. Coarse flat coat with invisible undercoat. Black with clear tan markings. Tail usually docked.

A strong powerful dog which only those experienced with dogs should take on. Good early upbringing is essential. Needs lots of exercise and understanding.

DOBERMANN PINSCHER

Invented in the 1880s by Herr Louis Dobermann in Germany. He wanted a medium-sized dog to guard him while he was collecting taxes. The breeds he blended were probably the Rottweiler, Manchester Terrier and German Pinscher.

Intelligent, bold, alert, loyal, obedient and a devoted companion. Ever watchful. Probably the best guard in the world. Not a bully, but if attacked is unlikely to be the loser. Slightly standoffish with outsiders.

Almond-shaped eyes, matching coat. Small, neat ears. Long, lean neck. Square body. Short, firm back. Cat-like feet. Free, balanced movement. Smooth, short coat. Black, brown, blue or fawn (called Isabella) with rust red markings. Tail usually docked.

If brought up properly, a great family dog which will protect its owners to the death. Needs lots of exercise and firm but fair handling.

101

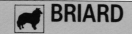

French sheepdogs have been around for centuries and the Briard is the most popular variety. They were used mainly as herding and guarding dogs and perhaps even for hunting in the distant past. The Briard is probably the most ancient French sheepdog.

Intelligent, happy dogs that should show no sign of nervousness or aggression. Very sensitive and with a little bit of work, obedient. Charming, gentle nature. Lots of energy that requires outlets in vigorous exercise.

Square muzzle. Dark brown eyes. Ears set high, when alert should swing slightly forward. Lips always black. Firm, level back. Slightly longer in back than height. Effortless movement. Long coat. Slightly wavy and very dry. All black, or with white hairs through coat. Fawn with dark shading or slate grey.

Coat needs a lot of attention. Needs lots of free running exercise. Guarding instinct present. Be very careful selecting a breeder. Hereditary eye and hip problems in this breed.

BLOODHOUND

Believed to have come to Britain with William the Conqueror. In the 8th century, Saint Hubert is said to have bred the ancestors of the Bloodhound for deer hunting and after his death, monks continued the breed and gave it his name.

A sensitive dog with an affectionate temperament. A one-man dog who is noble and dignified. Quite reserved and like all dogs bred for their scenting abilities suffers from temporary deafness, when in pursuit of an interesting aroma.

Narrow head, furnished with loose skin. When head carried low skin falls into ridges and folds. Dark brown or hazel eyes. Well-sprung ribs. Strong loins, deep and slightly arched. Long, thick, tapering tail carried like a scimitar. Smooth, weatherproof coat. Black and tan, liver and tan or red.

Needs free running exercise and careful training for obedience. A large dog that needs careful feeding to avoid stomach problems. Excessive wrinkling can cause problems.

IRISH SETTER
IRISH RED & WHITE SETTER No height or weight specified

By end of 16th century, Irish shooting spaniels had evolved.
Bloodhound blood was introduced to improve scenting ability.
Black pointers from Spain were imported and the longer-legged
Setter was born. Red and Whites slightly heavier than the Red.

Sweet, affectionate dogs. Given inadequate training and exercise
can result in the canine equivalent of the dizzy blonde. Energetic
and tenacious. Spirited and rather highly-strung. Quite
independent — training can be quite challenging.

Almond-shaped eyes. Deep chest. Ribs well-sprung. Straight
topline sloping gently to withers. Small feet. Free-flowing
movement. Short and fine coat on head, front of legs and tips of
ears. Elsewhere flat and free of wave. Rich chestnut. Rarer Red
and White — pearly white with solid red patches.

This is a challenging breed to train, so is perhaps not for the
first-time dog owner. Lovely nature. Some grooming needed and
lots of free exercise — if you can train them to come back!

Known in Britain since the 14th century and probably descended from the Spanish hunting dogs. Sir Edward Laverack spent 50 years improving the breed. Sir Purcell Llewellin used his strain to evolve the hunting and field trial strain.

Gentle, affectionate and patient nature. Intensely friendly and good-natured. Full of spirit and energy. Fond of children and thriving on human companionship. Needs company, should not be left alone for very long periods.

Head carried high. Oval eyes. Low-set velvety ears. Clean-cut neck. Short back. Slightly arched loins. Well-padded feet. Tail set almost in line with back, slightly curved. Free graceful movement. Slightly wavy coat. Black, orange, lemon or liver all with white flecks (belton means flecked) or tricolour.

Sweet-natured dogs with an independent streak. Need a lot of exercise and grooming. Gentle with children, but require lots of companionship and early training.

Most countries in Europe can claim an influence on this breed. When guns were introduced to Britain, this breed was developed to assist man in the new style of hunting. The first known dogs of the breed were called: Major, Drake, Hamlet and Bounce.

Very adaptable dog. Obedient and eager to please. Kind, even disposition. Aristocratic. Alert and never tiring. Intelligent and obedient. Quick to learn and very eager to please. Devoted, loyal and extremely sensitive.

Muzzle concave — dish-faced. Hazel or brown eyes. Kindly expression. Thin ears, lying close to head. Long muscular neck. Well-sprung ribs. Oval feet. Tail thick at root, should lash from side to side when moving. Fine, short coat. Lemon, orange, liver, black with or without white or tricolour markings.

Needs a great deal of activity to keep fit and happy. Minimal grooming. Not for families which don't enjoy the great outdoors. Given enough activity, a happy family member.

ALASKAN MALAMUTE

Probably gets its name from the Mahlemut people of North America. Highly prized by the Inuits and used to hunt polar bear and protect their caribou herds. Arctic explorers have used teams of this breed to pull their sleds on Polar expeditions.

Very loyal, excellent guard dog. Friendly with people, but not so accommodating with other dogs. Extremely intelligent and independent. Will think about commands before carrying them out. Very dignified, but playful and affectionate.

Broad head. Brown, almond-shaped eyes set obliquely. Small triangular ears. Strong body. Deep chest. Slightly sloping back. Protective hair between toes. High-set tail. Thick, coarse outer coat. Dense undercoat. Light grey to black or gold to red with white markings — or solid white.

One of the most ancient of breeds and rather a connoisseur's choice. His temperament means you need understanding and skill to train him. Needs lots of food, exercise and grooming.

RHODESIAN RIDGEBACK
61–69cm

Descends from dogs owned by the Hottentots before the 16th century in South Africa. When European settlers came their dogs interbred. Was known as the Lion Dog — also hunted buffalo, leopard and antelope in packs.

Dignified, intelligent. Aloof with strangers but should show neither aggression nor shyness. Totally devoted to his master. As a hunter, he would give his life to serve his owner — this quality is not lost. Gentle with his friends.

Ridge on the back is the distinctive feature. Caused by coat growing in the opposite direction. A clearly defined ridge is highly prized — should have two identical, but opposite crowns. Broad between the ears. Intelligent eyes. Chest deep. Loins strong and slightly arched. Light wheaten to red.

Hunting background can make this breed a bit of a handful with other dogs. Needs lots of exercise. Loyal and protective in the right hands.

A recent creation. Only recognized in Britain in 1924. Mr Mosely and friends interbred Mastiffs with Bulldogs creating a blend of 60/40. The aim was to produce a gamekeepers' dog to protect them from poachers unwilling to be caught alive.

Powerful, active and very dependable. High-spirited. Vigilant and faithful. Usually excellent with children. Full of character and dignity. An imposing guard, a very protective temperament and an impressive warning bark.

Powerful, but not cumbersome. Large square skull. Wrinkles when alert. Skull's circumference should equal height of dog to shoulder. Dark or hazel eyes. Teeth should meet squarely, but slightly prominent underjaw allowed. Cat-like feet. Strong tail. Any shade of brindle, fawn or red with a black muzzle.

Eats a great deal and needs reasonable exercise. A large dog that requires a good-sized car and other sizeable items. Calm and gentle with friends, needs careful upbringing.

109

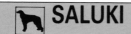 # SALUKI

58–71cm

At the time of the Crusades the Saluki was brought from the Middle East to Europe. These desert hunters — first registered as Persian Greyhounds — were highly prized and could only be given as a gift by their original Muslim owners.

Great companions although possessing hunting dog instincts. Very clean dogs. They should never be over-noisy or aggressive. Gentle and dignified. Happy to be with the family and rather standoffish with strangers. Very intelligent.

Long, narrow head. Large oval eyes. Long ears covered with silky hair. Chest deep and quite narrow. Slightly arched over loin. Two inner toes considerably longer than outer toes. Tail well-feathered. White, cream, fawn, golden red, tricolour, black and tan or grizzle.

A good, clean, gentle dog in the house, lacking doggie odour. Must have lots of free running exercise and attention to the coat on the ears, legs and tail. Perhaps not ideal with cats.

First used as gundogs in France, retrieving game from water. Poodle may originate from a German word meaning one who plays in water. The modern-day trim has developed from the functional clip which kept joints warm after swimming.

Intelligent companions — a real dog under the fancy coat. Happy dogs that are usually high-spirited and keen to play and entertain. A bit of a show off, very quick and keen to learn. A touch of mischief.

Long, fine skull. Almond-shaped eyes — full of fire. Head carried with dignity. Deep chest. Short back. Tight, well-cushioned feet. Sound, free movement. Profuse, thick and curly coat. All solid colours allowed — white, cream, brown, black, silver, blue, apricots etc. Tail set high and often docked.

A very large dog that enjoys free exercise. Coat does not shed so needs to be brushed and regularly clipped. The breed comes in two smaller sizes if you want the problem scaled down!

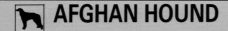

AFGHAN HOUND

64–74cm

Afghanistan royal family's hunting dog for centuries. Coursing hound that's been around for thousands of years. A very versatile dog — a capable herder and guard when the situation necessitates. Able to track prey over mountainous terrain.

Proud, aloof, very regal and dignified. Sometimes, however, cannot resist playing the court jester, pouncing and cavorting and acting the fool. Very independent and distant with strangers. Adores attention and affection.

Impression of speed with power. Skull long. Almost triangular eyes, slanting slightly upwards. Proud neck carriage. Level back. Hipbones rather prominent. Deep chest. Large feet. Tail with a ring at the end. Springy movement. Long, fine coat. All colours acceptable.

Needs a lot of grooming and exercise. Independent character — can make training them to come when called a nightmare. Coursing instinct means cats and squirrels aren't safe.

Largest Japanese breed and known to exist in polar regions for at least the last 300 years. Ownership used to be the preserve of royalty who used it to hunt wild boar, deer and the Japanese Black Bear. Name stems from the Japanese province of Akita.

Dignified, courageous and very dominant. Highly intelligent and an affectionate companion. Loyal and protective. In Tokyo there is a statue to commemorate an Akita called Hachiko who kept a 9 year vigil for his dead owner. Can be difficult with other dogs.

Large, broad head. Large black nose. Quite small almond-shaped eyes. Small, thick triangular ears. Strong jaws. Longer in body than height at the shoulders. Level back. Skin pliant, not loose. Thick feet. Large, full tail curled over back. Coarse outer coat. Soft undercoat. Any colour providing brilliant and clear.

An athletic dog that needs a lot of exercise. Not easy to train, as it has a streak of independence. Probably not for those without considerable experience of dogs.

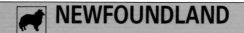

No one can be sure of the Newfoundland's past. Some say it was the only breed native to North America — others claim it as a descendant of Pyrenean Mountain Dogs brought over by emigrating French fishermen. A sea-rescue and draught dog.

Gentle giant. Very docile. Gentle and patient and somewhat paternal towards smaller animals. Loyal and deeply attached to his owner. Lord Byron wrote of his Newfie "all the virtues of a man without his vices." Natural life-saving instinct.

Broad and massive head. Small, dark brown eyes. Small ears. Strong neck. Large, webbed feet. Slight rolling gait. Double coat. Dull black with bronze tinges or chocolate colour with a splash of white permitted on chest, toes and tip of tail. White dogs with black marking are called Landseers, after the painter.

Needs lots of exercise and swimming if possible. Terrible dribblers and their coat can moult in extraordinary quantities. Select line with good hip dysplasia record. Food bill hefty.

Tibetan Mastiffs and Molossian Hounds thought to be ancestors of the breed. Romans probably brought the dogs to Spain and then over the mountain ranges of Europe and Asia. Used to guard sheep, often running in pairs, wearing spiked collars.

Gentle, but still with a strong guarding instinct. Family dog rather than a one-man friend. Affectionate and tolerant with children. Intelligent and slightly independent. Quick to learn, but not always so quick to obey. Gets on with most animals.

Immense size and substance, but still elegant. Almond-shaped, amber eyes. Intelligent expression. Small, triangular ears. Roof of mouth and lips mainly black. Profuse, fine undercoat — longer outercoat. Mainly white with or without patches of badger, wolf-grey or pale yellow.

Lots of exercise, grooming and food needed. Enjoys family life, but isn't really suited to normal indoor life. Lovely character but few people have the lifestyle to fit this dog.

In mid-17th century used as a watchdog in the Hospice of Saint Bernard in the Swiss Alps. Probably descended from the Molossian. Proved to be excellent pathfinders and displayed natural life-saving ability in fog and snow.

Unusually graceful for such a large dog and possessing tremendous dignity. Faithful and gentle, especially patient with children. Very intelligent, steady and reliable. Courageous, kindly and extremely trustworthy.

Massive skull — circumference more than double length. No excessive haw showing. Long, thick muscular neck. Broad back. Heavily boned legs. Easy movement. Rough coats: dense and flat. Smooth coats: close and hound-like. Orange, mahogany or red brindle with white markings.

Need lots of space to exercise properly. Take expert advice on feeding, particularly during rapid growth. Find a breeder with good hip dysplasia record. Terrible dribblers.

Tall, coursing hounds were always the favourites of the princes of Imperial Russia. Selective breeding produced a fast, intelligent dog which could catch a wolf and hold it down until his master approached. Also known as a Russian Wolfhound.

Cool and reserved with strangers. Their aloofness should not be confused with shyness. Affectionate to those chosen to be friends. Intelligent but very independent with a touch of arrogance. Sometimes stubborn. Not ideal with children.

Graceful, aristocratic and elegant. Long, lean head. Bones and veins are clearly visible. Dark, almond-shaped eyes. Small, delicate ears. Neck slightly arched. Great depth of chest. Back rather bony, rising in a graceful curve. Loins broad, powerful. Long, low-set tail. Silky, flat or rather curly. Any colour.

Needs space to gallop. Coat needs attention and feeding must be carefully supervised to prevent problems in rapid growth phase. Not good with cats or small children.

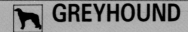

Mentioned in the Bible, Book of Solomon chapter XXX verses 29–31. Probably has a Middle East origin. Always prized as a speedy hunting dog capable of out-running fox, hare and even stag. Gaze-hounds, dogs which hunt by sight rather than scent.

Slightly aloof with strangers but devoted to the family. Sensitive, gentle and quite content to curl up and doze for most of the day — so long as it is in a warm spot. However, hunting instinct makes co-habitation with cats difficult.

Show and racing dogs quite different. Show ones tend to be larger and slightly heavier than their fleet-of-foot relatives. Bright, oval eyes. Rose-shaped ears. Long, muscular neck. Deep chest. Slightly-arched loin. Long tail, slightly curved. Black, white, red, blue, fawn, fallow, brindle with or without white.

Don't need as much exercise as many imagine. As a result, ex-racers are always desperate for a home. They can make excellent pets even for flat-owners, providing they don't have cats!

DEERHOUND

Middle Eastern traders probably brought the Greyhound to Britain 3,000 years ago. As the dogs moved north, hunting deer, could have developed rougher coats to cope with cold weather. Some think they're a descendant of the Irish Wolfhound.

Gentle and friendly. Eager to please. Affectionate, loving and devoted to their owners. Intelligent, calm and very forgiving. A reproachful look is his only likely mode of defence. Fairly easy to train — but hunting instinct difficult to suppress.

Long, flat skull. Slightly aquiline nose. Dark eyes. Far-away look when roused. Ears set high. Good reach of neck, nape obvious. Deep, rather than broad back. Well-arched loin. Shaggy coat, crisp to the touch. Dark blue-grey, brindle, yellows, sandy-red or red fawns with black points.

Needs open spaces to stretch out in. Coat needs regular attention. Prefers cold to heat. Careful feeding needed during rapid growth. Needs less food than most dogs of this height.

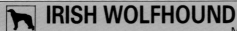

Used in Ireland to hunt wolf, boar, stag and elk. Flourished up to the 16th century but wolves then became extinct. In 1652, Irish parliament passed a law banning the export of the Irish Wolfhound as their numbers had dropped to dangerous levels.

Very willing to please, tremendously gentle and sensitive. Friendly and affectionate and full of character and dignity. Calm and reliable. Patient with children and other animals. Quiet and laid-back to the point of laziness.

Long head. Dark, oval eyes. Rose-shaped ears of dark colour. Very deep chest. Long back, arched loins. Long, slightly curved tail. Rough coat on body, legs and head. Especially wiry over eyes and under jaw. Grey, brindle, red, black, pure white, fawn, wheaten and steel grey.

High purchase price, feeding bills and a short life-expectancy may be off-putting. You'll need a large car, too. Surprisingly good pets with careful feeding and reasonable exercise.